Living the Jesus Prayer

Irma Zaleski

D1054022

NOVALIS

CONTINUUM • NEW YORK

Novalis   The Continuum Publishing Company
49 Front St. East, 2nd Floor   370 Lexington Avenue
Toronto, Ontario   New York, NY 10017
Canada M5E 1B3   U.S.A.

© 1997 Irma Zaleski
Published in Canada by Novalis, Saint Paul University, Ottawa,
Canada, and in the U.S.A. by the Continuum Publishing Company.
Published in the U.K. by Gracewing (Fowler Wright Books)

Second printing 1998

Cover: Icon painted and photographed by Marysia Kowalchyk for the
chapel of St. John the Compassionate, Toronto, Canada.
Cover design: Kim Lee Kho and Kal Honey

Canadian Cataloguing-in-Publication Data
Zaleski, Irma, 1931-
        Living the Jesus prayer
Rev. ed.
ISBN 2-89088-792-8
        1. Jesus prayer. 2. Spiritual life – Christianity
I. Title.
BV260.Z34 1996   248.3'2   C96-900583-0

Library of Congress Cataloguing-in-Publication Data
Zaleski, Irma.
        Living the Jesus prayer / Irma Zaleski.
        p. cm.
        ISBN 0-8264-1090-1
        1. Jesus prayer. I. Title.
BT590.J28Z35   1998
242'.7–dc21   97-50155

Printed in Canada

Contents

Foreword

I was introduced to the practice of the Jesus Prayer many years ago by Father B, a Catholic priest. One day he explained to me briefly the tradition of the Prayer and suggested that I try praying it.

It was a strange and difficult time for me. I had just returned to the practice of the sacraments after twenty years' absence. I was still deeply grateful for the grace, but I was also beginning to face the reality of the new life that I had embraced. Old habits, demands of everyday living, old relationships and interests were reasserting themselves, and doubts were beginning to assail me. At the moment of conversion, I was sure that I had met Christ and that I had experienced his presence and his mercy, but, as usually happens, that experience soon paled and seemed less real.

I had no habit of prayer and no clear understanding of what the spiritual life really was. Above all, I had very little understanding of the infinite, unconditional mercy of God, and therefore I had no way of relating to my own poverty and weakness without being crushed by guilt. I kept trying to justify myself, to be "good," to appear "blameless" before God and others. As my inability to do so became clearer and clearer to me, the temptation to discouragement and despondency was very strong.

It was at this point that I began to pray the Jesus Prayer. I took it up without having any clear idea of what it was all about, of where it would lead me. I was soon bored with it and wondered what the point was, but somehow, through the grace of God, I kept going. Eventually, I began to realize that the essential truth of our faith, the Good News – proclaimed to us from the beginning, but which sometimes takes us a life-time to grasp – was not that we were suddenly made perfect and free from all danger of sin, but that the infinite source of God's mercy and love had been opened to us in Christ. The Jesus Prayer became for me a true healing expression of the reality of my relationship with God.

This little book is an attempt to share this great gift. Nothing in it is my own invention. Everything I learned from others, from my spiritual directors, from reading, from friends walking the same path. The only thing which is truly mine is the experience of "failure" – my inability to pray "well" – and the gratitude for the grace of perseverance in praying it "badly," for the glimpse of the life to which the practice of the Jesus Prayer may lead those who embrace it.

The Prayer

The Jesus Prayer, or alternatively, "the Prayer of Jesus," also referred to as "the prayer of the Name of Jesus," "unceasing prayer," "prayer of the heart," or "prayer of silence," is an ancient form of prayer, of being *attentive* to God, practised in the early Church and carried on to the present day by an unbroken tradition. Till recently, it has been mainly used by the Eastern Church, but it is now also becoming known to increasing numbers of Christians in the West. It began in the early centuries of Christianity, as a prayer of monks and nuns, Fathers and Mothers of the Desert, but was soon taught to everyone who was drawn to it, and is now practised by thousands of men and women, lay as well as religious, all over the world.

Its form is very simple. It consists of the constant repetition of just a few words: "Lord Jesus Christ, Son of God, have mercy on me, a sinner," or "Lord Jesus Christ, have mercy on me," or "Lord Jesus, have mercy," or even of the single word, "Jesus." The exact formula does not matter as long as the Holy Name of Jesus is central to it. But once we find the exact wording which speaks to us most, we should stay with it. Our practice of the prayer is easier and takes root in us sooner if we do not keep on "experimenting" with it. We practice it by sitting still, with our eyes closed, and repeating the words slowly, gently, attentively, and silently, over and over again, not so much with our lips as with our minds.

Some teachers of the prayer recommend that the words should be synchronized with the rhythm of our breathing (e.g., "Lord Jesus Christ" breathing in, and "have mercy on me," breathing out). This helps to still the mind and allows the words of the Prayer to flow in and out in a very natural way. But it is better not to worry too much about it. If we practise saying the prayer regularly, this synchronization tends to happen of its own accord. It is important not to concentrate on the method, the technique of the prayer, but merely say the words as simply and as attentively as we can.

This applies equally to the choice of position we adopt while saying the prayer. It is best to sit up straight, for the simple reason that it is easier to be alert and stay awake that way. Apart from that, position does not matter. The Fathers usually stood while praying; others sat, knelt or prostrated themselves. St. Francis of Assisi often prayed lying on his back. We should choose a position which is best for us, which makes it easier for us to stay attentive. And again, as we continue praying the Jesus Prayer and it begins to establish itself in us, as we begin to realize more and more to whom we are being attentive, we shall find out for ourselves what is our best position for prayer; our bodies will spontaneously assume a position which best expresses our awareness of being in the presence of God and opening our hearts to his mercy.

Prayer of the Heart

The Jesus Prayer is also referred to as prayer of the heart. It rises from the deepest place of our being, from its very centre, for that is what *the heart* means, not our physical heart. It is therefore sometimes said that while saying the words of the prayer we should "seek our hearts," we should try and "enter our hearts," or "put our heads in our hearts" and say the words there. But this is not necessary and should not be undertaken without the advice and guidance of an experienced spiritual director. It may easily lead to preoccupation with technique and involve us in all sorts of fantasies. We say the words of prayer not to ourselves, but to Jesus, who is right there with us, closer than we can possibly imagine. The presence of Jesus with us is a fact – as he has promised. Christ *is* with us; we do not need to do anything to bring it about. All we need to do is to be open to him. If we just keep saying the words of the prayer to him in whom we believe, we will find our true hearts without any self-conscious effort to do so. We will become aware that our hearts are burning within us, just as did the hearts of the disciples on the road to Emmaus.

Beginning the Jesus Prayer

How does one decide to begin praying the Jesus Prayer? In a way, one doesn't. One is led to it by the Holy Spirit. In this sense, it can be seen as a "vocation," a path of life, always initiated by God, a response to a call. As St. Paul wrote to the Corinthians, to say "Jesus is Lord" is possible only for those who are moved to it by the Holy Spirit (1 Corinthians 12:13). It is the result of the Spirit "groaning" in us (Romans 8:26). All true prayer is not of our own invention. It is our surrender to the Spirit of Jesus praying in us to the Father, in ways which we cannot understand, but with which we can unite. That is why the Jesus Prayer is also called the Prayer of Jesus.

This is very, very important. To start the practice of the Jesus Prayer – of any prayer – and, above all, to persevere in it, we must be drawn to it by the Holy Spirit. Each time we pronounce the Name of Jesus, we are doing so as a gift of the Holy Spirit, the fruit of our redemption. We are, in a very real sense, opening ourselves to the incarnation of Jesus in us, through the Holy Spirit. We are becoming like the Mother of God, God-bearers.

How do we know that we are called to this way of prayer? The only answer is that, if we feel drawn to try it, we should try it. It doesn't really matter what our motives are. If our motives are not pure (and whose ever are?), God will purify them. If it is not God's will for us, we shall not persevere, but, if it is, we shall soon know. The Jesus Prayer, like any true call, any vocation, any true love, is never imposed on us; it never does violence to our deepest spiritual desires and longings but fulfils them. Nobody else can ever tell us how we must pray. Somebody may suggest a way to us – our spiritual director, if we have one, may encourage us to try it – but, in the end, it is between us and God. There are many ways in which God may want to lead us to experience his presence in our hearts, and the Jesus Prayer is one of them. If it is for us, we should embrace it gladly, but we must never say that it is the only way, or that it is a better way than others. All we need to know is that it is for us.

The Discipline

At first, the prayer will cost us some effort and discipline, and it is important, especially in the beginning, to set aside some time for it (perhaps twenty minutes, or half an hour) every day, twice a day if at all possible. We should not be too concerned if our attention wanders, if we forget what we are saying, if we are distracted or even bored. We just return to saying the prayer, and keep saying it through the whole period we set aside for it. It is important not to force ourselves beyond our limits, not to make an obligation of it, a burden we cannot carry. Pushing ourselves a little is all right, and at times even necessary, but we should be gentle with ourselves. To pray the Name of Jesus is a privilege, and will soon become a joy.

We must not confuse this joy with pleasant experiences or feelings. It is, in fact, very important not to expect to experience anything, to feel anything, to have any "insights" as the result of our prayer. The Fathers tell us that any thoughts that come to our minds while we are praying (and there will be many – good and bad, profound and silly) are a distraction, products of our own minds. The work of the Jesus Prayer is to silence our minds. As soon as we realize that we are thinking about something, we should let go of our thoughts and gently return to saying our prayer.

The same discipline is necessary regarding our feelings and imagination. We should not try to imagine that we see Jesus or to feel his presence; we should not try to picture him at all. We should not try to do anything, except simply repeat the words of the prayer and believe that he is always present as he has promised.

> We are taught, when reciting the Jesus Prayer, to avoid as far as possible any specific image or picture. . . . The Jesus Prayer is not a form of imaginative meditation upon different incidents in the life of Christ. But, while turning aside from images, we are to concentrate our full attention upon, or rather within, the words. The Jesus Prayer is not just a hypnotic incanta-

tion but a meaningful phrase, an invocation addressed to another Person . . . . And so the Jesus Prayer should not be said mechanically, but with inward purpose; yet at the same time the words should be pronounced without tension, violence, or undue emphasis . . . .[1]

This is not easy. The discipline of the Jesus Prayer, if taken up seriously, soon loses the excitement of all new beginnings. At times, it may seem monotonous, frustrating, even boring. Our bodies do not like sitting still; our minds do not like having to fast from thinking; our emotions do not like being disregarded. We crave a change, something new and more exciting. That is the time for faith and perseverance. Perhaps we might remind ourselves that anything worth doing at times seems monotonous and pointless, a grind, but that only if we persevere in it can we experience the joy of its fruits. Sometimes, of course, we need to take a break, draw a deep breath, go for a walk, read a book, do whatever we do to relax. We shall probably find that while we are walking, reading, or just breathing, the prayer still goes on in our hearts. We can't get away from it!

Distractions

Perhaps the greatest difficulty most of us face in our practice of the Jesus Prayer, and the greatest cause of discouragement, are the distractions which we seem never able to avoid. It may often appear to us that, however hard we try, we cannot pay attention to the words of the prayer even for a minute. It is a constant temptation to conclude that we "just can't do it," that this way of praying is not for us. This is why the teachers of the Jesus Prayer always seek to warn us of this danger and reassure us that distractions are of no importance. They are like passing waves on the surface of our minds, or clouds drifting across a clear sky – they do not ever obscure the presence of God before the eyes of our heart. At first we must simply take this truth on faith, but eventually, God willing, we shall experience it.

It has been said that distractions, rather than being obstacles to our practice of prayer, can become a powerful instrument of our growth in it. Our inattention may become the means of *calling us to attention* – of reminding ourselves, moment by moment, of the real meaning of the words we are trying to say, the means of our moment-by-moment conversion. Each time we return to the prayer, each time we become aware of how we "failed" in it, we become more aware of our weakness and of our need of God's love and mercy.

We must never worry whether we are saying the prayer well or not so well, attentively or distractedly, with energy, or half-asleep. Often, after what we might consider a completely "unsuccessful" period of prayer, we find ourselves most at peace and closest to God. The Prayer of Jesus is always God's work in us; it is Christ's work, not ours. We just say the prayer and stay as quiet and as open as we can.

Unceasing Prayer

Apart from those special times we set aside for it, we may say the words of the prayer at any other moment we find ourselves remembering it. In fact this is how many people first start on the path of the Jesus Prayer – simply saying it when they remember to say it. If we do that, we will be surprised how often these moments occur: in bed before we go to sleep, waiting for the bus, washing the dishes, having a shower, gardening, driving to work, or walking. Soon (for some of us, perhaps, this happens not so soon – it does not matter, it is up to God) the words of the prayer will penetrate our minds and hearts, and will continue sounding silently within us, of their own volition as it were. We will find ourselves saying them without any conscious effort, first thing in the morning, and last thing at night. They will become one with the rhythm of our breathing and the beating of our heart. They will become part of us. We will then discover the great secret of unceasing prayer about which St. Paul spoke (2 Thessalonians 5:17).

People who are drawn to the Jesus Prayer often have a desire to "pray always," to pray unceasingly. Perhaps they have come across these words of St. Paul or heard somebody speak about them, or read about them, but one way or another they become conscious of a desire to learn how to pray always. Perhaps they have tried various ways to achieve it, and sought the advice of various spiritual teachers. But they are never satisfied, never quite convinced. Then, somehow, they are introduced to the Jesus Prayer and find that it truly answers their need. This is well illustrated by a Russian story published in English under the title, *The Way of the Pilgrim,* which has played a very important part in spreading the knowledge of the Jesus Prayer in the West.

The book is a story of a simple pilgrim in nineteenth-century Russia, who describes how he learned about the Jesus Prayer. He tells us that one day, when he was in church on the Feast of Pentecost, St. Paul's Second Epistle to the Thessalonians was read, urging them "to pray without ceasing." These words had a profound effect on him. He was filled with a desire to find out how it could be done. He left his native village and travelled all over Russia. He searched out spiritual teachers, heard many sermons, but none of them could tell him how he could pray always.

Then one day, walking along a road, he met an old man, a monk from a nearby monastery, who invited him to come with him and rest awhile from his travels. The pilgrim thanked him, but said that he did not need to rest, but to find spiritual teaching.

"What sort of spiritual teaching are you searching for?" asked the old monk. "What is puzzling you?"

"Well, it is like this, Father," said the pilgrim. "About a year ago, while I was at the Liturgy, I heard a passage from the Epistles which bade men pray without ceasing . . . . This surprised me very much, and I was at a loss to understand how it could be carried out, and in what way it was to be done. A burning desire and thirst for knowledge awoke in me. Day and night the matter was never out of my mind. So I began to go to churches and to listen to sermons. But however many I heard, from not one of them did I get any teaching about how to pray without ceasing. They always talked about getting ready for prayer, or about its fruits and the like, without teaching one how to pray without ceasing, or what such prayer means. . . . I have not reached the understanding I longed for, and so to this hour I am still uneasy and in doubt."

Then the old man crossed himself and spoke:

"Thank God, my dear brother, for having revealed to you this unappeasable desire for unceasing interior prayer. Recognize in it the call of God and calm yourself . . . ."[2]

The pilgrim agreed then to come to the monastery with the old monk who introduced him to the practice of the Jesus Prayer. The rest of the book tells of his experiences as the practice of the prayer took hold of him, and as he travelled across Russia on foot, visiting many holy shrines, meeting many people, and always praying the Jesus Prayer and teaching others about it.

Guidance

The story of the Russian pilgrim also illustrates the fact that it is very difficult to walk the path of the Jesus Prayer, to persevere in the discipline, alone. That is why it is important to have a guide, a spiritual director, or a good confessor, someone experienced in the difficulties and demands of the path, someone willing to walk before us. All teachers of the prayer agree on that. It is not easy, however, for most people in the West to find such an experienced guide. Often we must do our best on our own. We practise the prayer, ask God constantly for guidance, go to confession when we can, perhaps find some help in reading. And, above all, we trust that Christ whose Name we constantly invoke, whose mercy we confidently expect, will guide us himself.

Praying the Jesus Prayer is a journey which we never make really alone. Mother Maria Gysi has said, "It is a journey, the soul must make it step by step and Christ leads the soul."[3] We trust that he will eventually lead us into the great silence of his presence, that he, who commanded the waves to be still, will himself bring peace to our turbulent minds.

Silence of the Heart

True silence is a great gift of God, and we should pray for it every day. It allows us to experience and hear God who lives in our hearts and is speaking to us. He is always there, and he is always speaking to us, but the outer and inner noise that usually fills our lives prevents us from hearing him. True silence is not merely an absence of noise – an external, physical silence, although, of course, that is also very important and at times necessary. True silence, the silence which the Jesus Prayer seeks to establish in us, is above all an inner silence, a silence of the heart.

True silence is the search of man for God. True silence is a suspension bridge that a soul in love with God builds to cross the dark, frightening gullies of its own mind, the strange chasms of temptation, the depthless precipices of its own fears that impede its way to God. . . .

Such silence is holy, a prayer beyond all prayers, leading to the final prayer of constant presence of God, to the heights of contemplation, when the soul, finally at peace, lives by the will of him whom she loves totally, utterly, and completely.[4]

To become still in order to hear God, to experience his presence, to be established in his silence, is the true aim of all Christian prayer. Christian prayer is never a program of self-improvement, "raising one's consciousness" or becoming "enlightened." It is not – at least not mainly – a list of petitions and requests for ourselves or others. It is a path of self-denial, of *kenosis*, a Greek word meaning "emptying," which St. Paul used about Christ in the second chapter of his Letter to the Philippians (vv. 6-11). It is a path of stripping ourselves of all that is not God, of becoming poor in heart so that God can fill us with himself, that we can be one with him.

This is also the aim of the Jesus Prayer. By repeating the Name of Jesus over and over and over again, by patiently putting away from us all distractions, all our own thoughts and feelings, our minds become emptied, purified, ready to receive the gift of silence, the gift of being still. We become aware of the great silence at the heart of our being, the silence behind the distractions, the noise, the emotions which assail us from all sides. We become aware of the Presence which this silence brings.

Desire for the Presence of God

The desire for inner stillness, for the silence of the heart, is really the desire to experience the presence of God, a longing to know that Jesus truly lives with us, is present with us, is always there for us. One of the great tragedies of our lives, of the lives of so many Christians, is not to experience that presence. So our faith never becomes truly real for us. We do what is required of us, but our hearts are not touched, we do not know the joy of it. And yet, this is why Christ came, why he suffered, died and rose again, why he sent us the Holy Spirit – to be always present with us. This is the meaning of the mystery of his mystical Body, the Church. This is the meaning of the sacraments, the meaning of our salvation in Jesus, of the coming of the Kingdom, and of the promise of Heaven.

How can this desire for the presence of Jesus be fulfilled? Only through prayer. This kind of prayer is usually called "contemplative" and is often considered possible only for a few "chosen" souls, mostly nuns and monks, and not for ordinary lay people. But this is not true. Contemplative prayer is for everyone.

A story is told about an old parishioner of St. Jean Vianney (the Curé of Ars) who used to spend a lot of time alone in church. St. Jean became curious about him and asked him one day, "Why do you spend so much time sitting in church? What do you think about?" The old man answered, "Oh, I just look at him, he looks at me, and we are happy together."

This wonderful story illustrates two important points about "contemplative" prayer: that it is not complicated, but is a simple way of being in the presence of God, and that one does not have to go to the desert or enter a monastery to experience it. But most of us, like the Russian pilgrim, need to find a path of prayer, a simple way of experiencing the presence of God and remaining in it. The Jesus Prayer can be such a way. It can become for us a means of entering the Kingdom of Heaven, of finding heaven on earth, for, as Blessed Elizabeth of the Trinity has said, "Heaven is God and God is in my heart."

This may seem to be a contradiction, for did we not say that experiences should never be sought? This is true. But, as we have already pointed out, the experience of the presence of God in Christ is not a matter of our own thoughts, our own feelings or imagination. It is a matter of awareness.

This awareness is a very simple one. We do not try to imagine that Jesus is there, even less what he looks like or what he says. We are simply aware of him the way we are aware of the presence of someone we love in the room next to us, or as a mother is always aware of what the children are doing, however busy she is. It is as simple as that. We know by faith that Jesus is here, is with us, and what we try to do is to remember it, to remind ourselves of it. That is all. The Jesus Prayer is a way of remembering. Not in the sense of bringing to mind a memory of something that is past, but of recalling, reminding ourselves of something that is present, that is right there with us. This remembering is the joy that the Jesus Prayer brings.

But this joy is not ours to summon at will, to grasp at as if it were a possession. Like the prayer itself, it is a gift. Ours is only a discipline of faith and perseverance. And the experience, the joy, when it comes, will come of its own accord, and will be nothing like whatever we could imagine. God is immensely bigger than our imaginations. Our hope is that when he comes, when he reveals himself to us, we will be able to recognize him, like the disciples who recognized him when he visited them after the Resurrection, in ways and at times they least expected.

Repentance

Another very important aspect of praying the Jesus Prayer is a readiness to accept the mercy of God. When we say the words "Have mercy on me, a sinner!" – for the prayer always implies those words, even if the form we actually use does not include them – we must be ready to recognize that we are, in fact, sinners in need of God's mercy. We can believe this. The Prayer of Jesus is a prayer of sinners, not of the virtuous:

> It is, in fact, exclusively for sinners. Awareness of our sinfulness is an indispensable prerequisite for saying the Prayer of Jesus. Without it real prayer is impossible for mortal flesh. To come to prayer with the notion that at a certain point we are "ready" . . . that we are worthy, is to put ourselves into a completely false relationship with the Absolute.[5]

At first it may be difficult to see how this could be a problem. Of course we are sinners, we have all sinned and it is likely we will sin again. And yet, if we are honest with ourselves, we will probably find that we have all sorts of reservations. Yes, we are sinners, but surely not all the time! Haven't we been forgiven? Must we harp on our sins "unceasingly"? Is it not a sign of an exaggerated, perhaps a neurotic sense of guilt? Of doubt in God's love for us? Lack of humility? Or even an expression of our rebellion against him who created us and who "saw that we were good"?

Many of these doubts and reservations are due to the fact that we do not understand sin in the same way as the early teachers of the Jesus Prayer understood it, and as the Tradition of the Church has always taught. When we think of sin, we think most often of our individual sins, our wrong deeds, sometimes of thoughts and desires, but mainly of deeds. We sin, we confess, we say we are sorry, we are forgiven, and the case is finished; there is no more sin (till next time). Repentance for us is simply an acknowledgement of the fact that we are human, imperfect, that we often fail at being "good." Anything more — true sorrow for our sins, tears of repentance, "doing penance" seems to us exaggerated and even obsessive.

The teachers of our Tradition saw it differently. When they talked about sin, they were thinking not so much of individual sins, but of their true source, of the condition of human beings who have turned away from God, whose love and attention are centred mainly on themselves rather than on God. In other words, it is the condition of those who are *off-centre,* who are not centred rightly, who are not in the right relationship with God. This is what sin really means. Sin, repentance, make no sense at all, except in the context of our relationship with God – as our failure in love. Viewed from that perspective, we are all sinners, because none of us can ever claim that we are truly centred, that we love God more than ourselves. None of us can say that we never think of ourselves first. To admit that we are sinners is not a question of neurotic feelings of guilt, a way of assigning blame, but a question of being real. It is also a way – a Christian's way – of approaching the great mystery of evil.

The Mystery of Evil

The reasons why we are the way we are, why we are so often imperfect, confused, unhappy, why we hurt ourselves and others, are very difficult, perhaps even impossible, to understand. The existence of evil – in ourselves and in the world – remains always an agonizing mystery, a question which often torments us. Our response can only be an act of faith – of trust in the ultimate victory of God's love – and of compassion for ourselves and others. But how hard that is, when faced with some unspeakable evil, some terrible act, perhaps a memory of something we have done, or failed to do! Even more difficult to bear, perhaps, is the constant, ever-present awareness of our "ordinary" lack of perfection, our failures in love, our weakness, our abysmal poverty. Praying the Jesus Prayer, calling ceaselessly upon God's mercy, may be the only way in which we can face the reality of who we are, find healing for our pain, and learn compassion for ourselves and for the world.

Only God Is Good

The Jesus Prayer, because it is a path of reality, is a way of learning – and accepting – the tremendous truth, too often forgotten, that "only God is good." We cannot be "good" because we do not really know what *good* is. We can never comprehend the nature of his infinite goodness and his infinite love. Strictly speaking, we cannot be "like him" – no effort of our own can ever make us so. It is, I think, true to say that as we walk the way of prayer, as we become more open to God, as we grow closer to him, we become more and more aware of how great an abyss separates us from him. We begin to understand why it was the greatest saints who seemed to mourn most deeply the fact that they were sinners. We begin, perhaps, to have a glimpse of the "inexpressible longing" for holiness, for wholeness, which made them so aware of their human failings – however small they may seem to us – and of their poverty before the holiness of God. It is this longing for God, this awareness of separation from him, which is the heart of true repentance. It is also the heart of the Jesus Prayer. It is a hard way, a painful way, but it is the way of truth and therefore of joy.

A Hymn of Joy

The Jesus Prayer, we are taught, is a great hymn of joy, because it acknowledges and proclaims our total trust in God's mercy, our conviction that he will never "get tired" of forgiving us and loving us. When we pray to him ceaselessly for mercy, we express our firm hope that he will save us and will draw us away from the unreality of sin into his own glorious reality. Our cry for mercy is a cry for healing. It is an expression of our faith in the fact that, though we are helpless to save ourselves from our preoccupation with self, from our fears, our sin, he will do it for us. He himself will bridge the abyss that separates us from him – he has already bridged it in Christ! The Jesus Prayer is our hymn of gratitude for the gift of salvation in Jesus. The Fathers called it a "summary" of the whole Gospel. The words, "Lord, Jesus Christ, Son of God, have mercy on me, a sinner!" are our joyful confession of faith in the truth of our salvation.

The Offering

When we say the Jesus Prayer, we stand empty-handed, having nothing of ourselves to offer, and expecting everything from God. That is why it has been compared to the Eucharist. This does not mean, of course, that it is of the same nature as the Eucharist, or that it could ever be viewed as a substitute for the Eucharist, but only that it resembles it in one respect. The Eucharist is the great, incomparable sign of the mystery of salvation and it is always the work of God. At the Eucharist everything is done *for* us, everything is offered *to* us; we cannot lay claim to having any part in it, except the offering of ourselves. We often find it difficult to accept this truth, because it seems to imply that nothing we do is of any value, and that we must remain totally passive in the work of our redemption. Everything we have to offer, everything we call "I" is so poor, so infinitesimally small in comparison to what we are receiving, that we hardly dare to offer it at all.

And yet, this offering of ourselves, however small and worthless it may seem, is of infinite value, because it constitutes our part in the work of salvation. It is our work: our part is not passive, but a vigorous taking up of our poor selves and offering them up to the mercy of God. It is an act of faith and therefore an act of thanksgiving, a *eucharist*, a hymn of praise for the mystery of salvation in Christ. Even a glimpse of that mystery makes our hearts overflow with gratitude and awe. When we pray the Jesus Prayer, we do the work to which we have been called, and we ceaselessly proclaim the same mystery, and offer the same worship of gratitude and awe. As the Letter to the Hebrews expresses it, through Jesus we offer to God "a continual sacrifice of praise, that is, the fruit of lips that confess his Name" (Hebrews 13:15).

Spiritual Communion

The Jesus Prayer has also been compared to Holy Communion. It is an act of our spiritual communion with Christ – of participation in his "perfect act of love." By repeating the name of Jesus, the Divine Word, we surrender ourselves totally to him, we throw ourselves completely on his mercy, we unite ourselves with him, we become aware that in a deep, true sense we can also say with St. Paul, "I live, but no longer I, but Christ lives in me" (Galatians 2:20).

Mother Maria put it this way:

The Jesus Prayer is understood best when it is considered in connection with the Eucharist, where we are permitted to join our self-surrender to Christ's perfect act of love . . . . In this self-offering . . . we are part of Christ, even before we receive him in Communion. Both self-oblation and communion are things which happen in eternity as well as in time. In the Eucharist, it is self-evident that Christ is all that we have and all that we are. He is, one might say, the perfect expression of the whole of our being as we desire it to be. Our thoughts, our will, all the words we could ever find to express ourselves are himself. Thus, in the Eucharist, as far as we offer ourselves, we are wholly simple; there we attain oneness. The practice of the Jesus Prayer, in which we allow Christ himself to be our prayer, is the abiding in this simplicity and oneness.[6]

The implications of this truth are greater than our minds can ever grasp or imagine. It means that all our lives, everything we do, say, think, even dream, everything we are, if surrendered to Christ, becomes united to him, and in a profound sense is an expression of his life, his action, his spirit. It means that all reality is sacramental, a sign of God's presence in the world, and that every moment of our lives, all our tasks however small – our "duty of the moment," as Catherine Doherty used to call it — are sacred and a prayer. *Our* prayer, but because we have surrendered all to Christ, also *his* prayer. In us Christ offers himself to the Father.

When we pray the Jesus Prayer, we become like the disciples, we *are* the disciples, who at the Last Supper heard the Priestly Prayer of Jesus for the first time (John 17). We realize that it is for us that he prays that we may be "established in his Name," and glorified with him. Of course, the Priestly Prayer of Jesus belongs to the whole Church, but perhaps in a very special way it belongs to those who are trying to surrender their whole lives, their whole being, to the power of the Name which the Father gave to his Son, and which lives in them.

When we are established in this Name, we are being glorified with him, we are becoming like him, we are participating in him. In the language of the Fathers we are being "divinized." As we continue to pray the Jesus Prayer, day after day, year after year, this tremendous truth penetrates our whole being, and our lives become more and more centred on it.

We Meet God Alone

There is still another dimension of the Jesus Prayer. Why, when we say the Jesus Prayer, do we say "have mercy on me, a sinner"? Why "me" and not "us"? Should we not pray for mercy for everybody? Should we not pray for the whole Church? Of course. In a very real sense every prayer is a prayer of the Church. Apart from the Church, the Body of Christ, our prayer means nothing. We cannot pray the Jesus Prayer outside the Church. When we say "Jesus" and call on his mercy, we ask for mercy on his whole body, the Church, and by implication on the whole of the redeemed universe (cf. Romans 8:21). But, because the Jesus Prayer is a prayer of repentance, the prayer of a sinner, it must also be a prayer of each one alone. In the final analysis, we have to make our own individual peace with God, find our own relationship with him, meet him face to face. Nobody can do it for us. Somebody can bring us to Jesus, but we must meet him ourselves. And nobody can ask forgiveness for our sins and be forgiven, but ourselves.

In this respect too, the Jesus Prayer resembles the sacraments. As we cannot be baptized by proxy, or go to confession for anybody else, neither can we receive Communion or any other sacrament for anyone but ourselves. We say "Jesus, have mercy on me," just as we say before Communion, "Lord, I am not worthy to receive you, but only say the word and I shall be healed."

Practice for Death

Mother Maria has also said that the Jesus Prayer puts us, as it were, in the spiritual space in which we shall find ourselves at the moment of death. We die alone. And the only other person there who will really matter at that moment will be Jesus, our Lord, our God, and our Judge. We shall have left everyone and everything else behind, we shall have crossed the boundary which separates life from death. We shall be judged according to "heavenly measures," which we cannot even begin to comprehend in this world, by Perfect Love, in the face of which we shall have nothing to offer but our weakness, our failure to love, and our repentance. We shall then, perhaps for the first time, truly understand the glory and the joy of repentance. We shall fully understand that in the presence of the perfect, inexhaustible love of God, we can never do anything but pray for mercy, and that we never need to do anything but pray for mercy. All of us, saints or sinners, at the end are like the Repentant Thief: we enter Paradise only through the mercy of Christ. When we realize that, we can truly rest; we finally find peace, the "peace of the End."[7]

The coming of that day, of our meeting with Christ face to face, is the only absolute certainty we have about the course of our lives, and it is already present in the mind of God. For God, all events of human life, every moment of time, is also an event in eternity, part of the eternal now. Thus, for God, our end is already known, his judgement has been already pronounced, and our cry for mercy has already been heard. His mercy has already flowed down on us and covered our wounds and misery. We have already been forgiven. We have already been raised from the dead. The Jesus Prayer places us in the reality of that moment, in the place of that meeting. When we say the Jesus Prayer, we are saying it for our end. In a very real sense we are *practising* for death.

This does not refer only to actual, physical death. Every Christian's life must also be a way of self-denial, of the daily death of self, because we must die to self in order to rise with Christ to new life. The Jesus Prayer, because it is a way of *kenosis*, of purification, is also a way of self-denial, of the death of self. Each time we call on Jesus to have mercy, we surrender ourselves to him, we accept his judgement and meet him in the "peace of the end." By praying the Jesus Prayer we are facing the fear of the end, but also beginning to experience the "indescribable and glorious joy" of our resurrection (1 Peter 1:3-9).

Victory Over Evil

The Jesus Prayer makes it possible for us to face all fear: the fear of death, but also the fear of life, of what life, what others can do to us. This is a true sign of victory over evil. The Gospel makes it absolutely clear that, if we become disciples of Christ, our task is to overcome evil, first of all in ourselves, but also in the world. But we must not do it as the world tries to do it, by returning evil for evil, by more anger, more violence, more hate. We are called to overcome evil as Christ did, by love and forgiveness, that is, by the power of his Cross and Resurrection. It is not by the fact of physical suffering alone, but by forgiving his tormentors, forgiving us all, that Christ vanquished evil and destroyed the power of death, and we are to do the same.

The greatest victory of evil consists in the reaction of fear and hatred which evil arouses in those who have been wronged. And its biggest defeat is when we refuse to react. We cannot overcome evil unless we first overcome, within ourselves, "the whole realm of re-action, re-sentment, re-venge."[8] The way of the Jesus Prayer is the way of overcoming this compulsion to react by surrendering all things, both good and evil, to Christ and asking him in his mercy to deal with them all. It does not matter what emotions may rage within us. Christian love is not an emotion, but an act of will. It is a way of opening ourselves to Christ's own love and mercy pouring into us and through us to others. When we do that, when we refuse to hate, but surrender all evil, all wrongs, to Christ's mercy, we deprive evil of the fruits of victory; we show in our own lives, in our suffering, that good is indeed stronger than evil, love infinitely more powerful than hate – that God can turn all evil into good.

Forgiveness – the refusal to turn away, to hate – is the essence of Christian love. As Christ has told us, even "pagans" can love those who love them. The challenge of Christian love is to love those who "hate and persecute" us. It is a most difficult, perhaps an impossible challenge: we fail it most often. But we are not discouraged – we never look for "success." We fail, we repent, and we try again and again – always holding on to the cloak of God's infinite mercy, always calling upon the power of his Name, always remembering that our victory, when it comes, will be not ours but his.

Christ Our Judge

Forgiving, calling on God's mercy for ourselves and all those who have sinned against us, or against whom we have sinned, is also a way of fulfilling Christ's commandment of not judging. All judgement has been given to Christ and we must not dare and presume to claim that right for ourselves. And this means first of all, perhaps above all, that we must not judge ourselves. We cannot judge ourselves because we can never fully understand what goes on in our heart, we cannot see ourselves as we truly are, as God sees us, as Christ sees us.

Does this mean that we are getting off easily? That, after all, our sins do not really matter, our wounds do not have to be lanced, our cancerous growths removed? Of course not. When we enter the path of the Jesus Prayer, we enter the path of repentance, of conversion and, as we begin to walk it, with each step we become more and more aware of our own pain, our own darkness, our own sin. And that is very hard for most of us. That is why this way has been called "white martyrdom." It is the way of the Cross, because there is no greater pain than to stand in the total poverty of our human weakness, to see clearly our misery, our inability to be "good." The temptation to judge ourselves, to hate ourselves, would be irresistible if we did not know and had not experienced the merciful, healing power of Jesus.

But because we have met Christ and have experienced his compassionate, loving presence, we can surrender all judgement to him and be at peace. We can accept ourselves as we are, we can love ourselves and also love others. For we have discovered that Christ's judgement is not the judgement of an inquisitor or a tyrant, but the judgement of the Good Physician. We go to him to show him our wounds, to tell him about our pains, our sins and failures, to let him see all the bleeding, cancerous places of our bodies and souls, not so that he may "punish" us, but that he may heal us. When we stand before him and say, "Lord Jesus, have mercy on me, a sinner!" we are not cringing in fear of punishment, but crying for help and healing. The Jesus Prayer teaches us to live the great mystery of our faith, the great paradox: we are called to repent always, but never to judge; to cry for mercy, but never to doubt God's forgiveness and love. It teaches us that to walk with Christ, to live in his presence, is to live in the presence of love.

The Work of Love

Because we cannot ever "see the heart" as God sees, we cannot really know what is good for us, and especially what is good for others. We don't know what their true needs are, what is the best solution for their problems, and what would assuage their pain. But we don't need to know. The Jesus Prayer can become for us a powerful way of intercession, of praying for others. By praying the Holy Name over them, we surrender each one of them to God's mercy and love and we trust that he himself will do what is best for them. In the words of Mother Maria:

> What can we do better than to commit all the names, one by one, into the Holy Name, thus bringing to Christ, with his own Holy Name, the immensity of human needs, that he himself in his sovereignty may unravel it and lead it towards the perfect solution?

She also quotes St. Catherine of Genoa who said that "she could never pray for this or that because she saw God already so busy in providing for each one the very best. All she could do was to present them all to him."[9]

When we intercede for others in this way, when we bring them all to the mercy of Christ – the good and the bad, those whom we love and those whom we cannot love, those who love us and those who hate us – we do what the Lord has told us to do and what he himself did on the Cross. This is the great way of love to which he has called us and also our work, the only work that truly matters, the work of love.

We sometimes worry that we are "not doing enough," not sharing enough, not serving the poor, visiting the sick, or performing other works of mercy. And, of course, it may very well be true. In order to be faithful to the Gospel, to fulfil the commandment of love, we must do what we can for each other. Without that we cannot call ourselves Christ's disciples. On the other hand, we often forget that our good acts will not bear much fruit, will not give life, if they are not performed out of love. And we cannot make ourselves love; it is a gift, the fruit of prayer, of opening our hearts to God. When we pray for others, we begin to love them as Christ loved them, and we do the work he commanded us to do. And if there is more we need to do, he will show it to us in his own good time.

By praying the Jesus Prayer over each human being we meet, by pronouncing the Holy Name over everything we do, over the whole natural world, over the whole universe, over the whole creation, we become instruments of their sanctification, channels of the Holy Spirit, bearers of the fire of Divine Love. And we ourselves "will go through the world with a new vision and with the new gift of our own heart. Thus we can (for he is in us) transform the world and make our own the words of Jacob to his brother: 'I saw your face, and it was as if I was seeing the face of God' (Genesis 33:10)."[10]

Living the Jesus Prayer

All that we have been taught about the practice of the Jesus Prayer, all that we have learned and experienced through it, will make us realize that it is much more than a "practice," a form of prayer and discipline. The Jesus Prayer is *a way of life*. Of course, it is a practice too. We need to make the effort, acquire the discipline, the *habit* of it. We struggle with its monotony, its demands to put away our own thoughts and feelings. We deny ourselves, we carry our daily cross of trying to do God's will and seeing more and more clearly how often we fail. We resist the temptation to judge ourselves, to judge anybody, to fight evil with its own weapons. But in the end, we do all that – we make the effort, accept the discipline, take up our cross – because we realize that it brings us life, that it is our life, the life to which we have been called. We *live* the Jesus Prayer.

Praying the Jesus Prayer, we enter a new world, a world of the real, constant Presence of the Risen and Glorified Christ. We live our lives, moment by moment, in a relationship with him. We take everything to him, we leave everything to him, we live everything in him. If we persevere, one day we shall open our eyes and see that, indeed, we have found the "hidden treasure," the pearl of great price, that we have already entered the Kingdom.

As has been said again and again, this life of intimate, constant, unceasing relationship with Jesus is not a question of thoughts or feelings, but of faith, and therefore a gift of God. There may be moments when we actually experience the reality of our life with Christ. These moments are a great joy, a special grace, a glimpse of heaven. But the essential thing is to keep that deep, central space of our being, which we call "the heart," wide open and turned towards him. The Jesus Prayer leads us into that space, and allows us to live there with him unceasingly.

The great teachers of our Tradition speak, with the boldness of their great faith and love, of the divinization of each human person, of being transfigured into that divine image which we were created to be. For those who are led to it and have the grace to persevere, the Jesus Prayer can be a path up the mountain of Transfiguration. God leading us, one day we too will reach the top of the mountain, the "place of the End," where we shall see him as he truly is, and become like him.

Notes

[1] Bishop Kallistos Ware, *The Orthodox Way*, St Vladimir's Seminary Press, Crestwood, N.Y., 10707, 1986, p. 164.

[2] *The Way of the Pilgrim*, translated by R. M. French, Seabury Press, 1968, pp. 5-7.

[3] Letter of September 3, 1974, *Mother Maria: Her Life in Letters*, ed. by Sister Thekla (Darton, Longman & Todd, London, 1979), p. 49. Mother Maria (Lydia Gysi), a great spiritual teacher and writer, was the foundress of the Orthodox Monastery of the Assumption in England. She died in 1977. Information about her published writings can be obtained from the monastery, Normanby, Whitby, North Yorkshire, Y0224PS, England, or from Peregrina Publishing Co., 17 Woodside Ave., Toronto, Ontario, Canada M6P 1L6.

[4] Catherine Doherty, *Poustinia (Christian Spirituality for Western Man)*, (Ave Maria Press, Notre Dame, Indiana, 1974). In this, her best-known work, the foundress of Madonna House Apostolate tried to explain Eastern Christian spiritual tradition to Western Christians (*Poustinia* is a Russian word meaning "the desert") Although her subject is not the prac-

tice of the Jesus Prayer as such, she refers to it repeatedly and puts it in the context of living the life of love, of total surrender to God.

5 "M.B.," "Hesychasm," *The Canadian Catholic Review,* Saskatoon, Sask., July 1988, p. 273.

6 Mother Maria (Lydia Gysi), *The Jesus Prayer,* The Library of Orthodox Thinking (Peregrina Publishing Co., 17 Woodside Ave., Toronto, Ontario, Canada M6P 1L6), 1991, p. 11.

7 Ibid., p. 38.

8 Ibid., p. 39.

9 Ibid., p. 15.

10 *Praying of the Name of Jesus,* by an Eastern Monk, John XXIII Centre for Eastern Studies, Fordham University Press, 1959, p. 8.